HARLEY-DAVIDSON

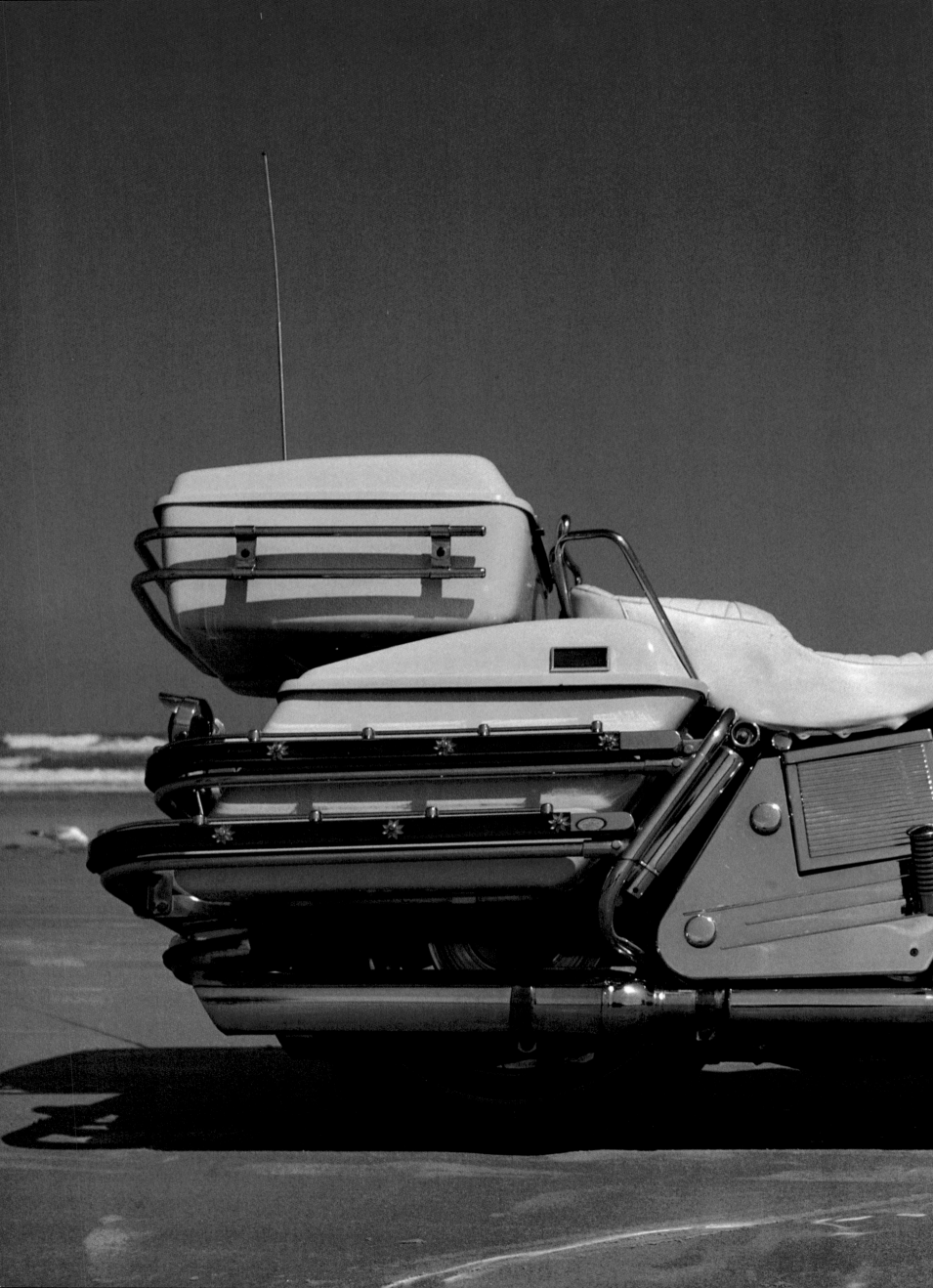

HARLEY-DAVIDSON

TONY MIDDLEHURST

MALLARD
PRESS

Produced by
Brompton Books Corporation
15 Sherwood Place
Greenwich, Connecticut 06830

Copyright © 1990 by Brompton Books Corporation

First published in the United States of America in 1990 by The Mallard Press
Mallard Press and its accompanying design and logo are trademarks of BDD Promotional Book
Company, Inc.

ISBN 0-792-45332-8

Printed in Italy

10 9 8 7 6 5 4 3 2 1

Page 1: Power and beauty...Rivera-carbed Evolution Low Rider ticks at rest after a leisurely cruise in the sun.

Pages 2-3: Archetypal Harley: the gold, chrome and white leather excess of a '76 Electra Glide in a classic setting – Daytona Beach.

Below: Everyone's dad knows at least one story about a guy who took despatches to the front line on one of these – the ever-dependable WLA45 (1942).

Contents

Introduction	6
Three Men and a Shed	8
Expression and Depression	16
Indian Troubles	34
Knuckleheads and Panheads	46
New Models and Economic Problems	62
The Best Harleys Ever?	80
Selected Specifications	110
Index and Acknowledgments	111

CC224044

TP16

Introduction

I'll never forget my first ride on a Harley.

It was the back end of the 1970's, when the summers seemed so much hotter and the roads so much more open. I was a callow youth then, still buzzing with the adrenalin – and the disbelief – that came from having landed a job as assistant road tester on a motorcycle magazine. I'd been 'broken in' on a succession of mind-numbingly quick Japanese superbikes, until finally I was ready to be trusted with my first 'hog' – a cherry red 1000cc Sportster.

Nothing that I had sampled before could have prepared me for the other-worldliness of that Sportster. Crimson peanut tank set off by acres of chrome, crude V-twin motor leaping about (rather alarmingly, it seemed) inside an impossibly spindly frame, freeway forks plunging and heaving in protest at the English A-roads, rock-hard seat and suspension pummelling my spine . . . Right then, the Sportster seemed about as inaccurately named as any motorcycle could be. Agricultural, noisy, thirsty, uncomfortable – it was the ultimate in excess. And I loved it.

I loved it even when, less than two miles into what was supposed to be an uplifting ride down to the Sussex coast (shared by an at first reluctant lady passenger), the clip holding the exhaust pipes together fell off. One piece of bent wire and several burned fingers later, the bike sounded disturbingly like an ailing World War II bomber, but at least we were rolling again. The lady was less than impressed, so I cut my losses and headed home. Just as well, since the clutch lever was so unbelievably heavy that I had been in some serious doubt about the long-term health of my left wrist.

Before the Evolution motor came along in the early 1980s, it had never been an easy job defending Harleys against their many detractors. Things are different now, of course. Now H-Ds can stand comparison with a surprisingly wide cross-section of competitors. But in nearly ninety years of continuous manufacture, the world's most famous and charismatic motorcycle company has always had a devout following among motorcyclists who recognise (and can afford to pay for) that certain indefinable quality which sets the Milwaukee machines apart from the rest.

In my time on *SuperBike* magazine, I lost count of the number of times photographic sessions involving test Harley-Davidsons were interrupted by members of the public. Misty-eyed men seemed to appear from out of nowhere, each of them with an H-D anecdote to retell. No other test bikes ever aroused anywhere near the same level of awed curiosity as Harleys did.

I always listened to those fellows, on the basis that I'll end up the same way when I'm an old man . . . and then I'll need someone to listen to *my* anecdotes.

Did I ever tell you about the time I was riding an '84 Low Rider across the Arizona desert, for example? Now, *that* was an adventure . . .

Left: Though the 'W' Sport Twin was a reasonable attempt at cashing in on a format which was popular in Europe, it proved too unexciting for the power-hungry USA market.

Right: Harley's big Milwaukee plant on Juneau Avenue, seen here in the latter part of the 1920s, was the subject of many expansion programs after its humble start in 1906.

Below right: Claude Temple enjoyed many successes on H-Ds outside of his own career as a motorcycle manufacturer. He won this 1921 Brooklands race at an average speed of 92.37mph.

whose prosperity had been founded on the relative cheapness of their products. The gradual weeding-out process affecting the weaker American marques gathered pace as war conditions severely restricted the importation from Europe of ancillary items not then produced by the native industry.

Indian, at that time the biggest motorcycle firm in America, suffered greatly in the war from self-inflicted wounds caused by the commitment of too great a proportion of their total output to military motorcycle production. In keeping with their conservative traditions, Harley-Davidson adopted a more circumspect posture. By offering a much smaller portion of their output to the government, they were able to maintain a healthy home market. Indeed, by exploiting Indian's short-sightedness, H-D were able to expand their agency network by poaching many of the Springfield company's under-supplied and understandably disaffected dealers.

When the war ended in 1918, Indian's home market had been effectively plundered. Harley-Davidson had improved their own position relative to Indian, such that the two companies were now very much on an equal footing with around 1000 dealers each. Detecting a bright future ahead, H-D's founders authorised another factory expansion programme in readiness for what they expected to be a doubling up of production from their sub-20,000 annual output during the straitened war years.

To take maximum advantage of the new trading conditions, the faithful old Model 9 single, the 'Silent Gray Fellow', was discontinued in 1918, to be re-placed in 1919 by a totally new model. The horizontally-opposed 37 cubic inch (600cc) Model W 'Sport Twin' was a Douglas lookalike, aimed squarely at Indian's highly rated Scout lightweight.

Unfortunately, and not for the last time, the market had been misjudged by Harley-Davidson. American motorcyclists were still in love with the big, fast 'Model J' V-twin. The Sport Twin was not what they wanted at that time, being rather slow and uninspiring. It sold reasonably well in H-D's recently created European export market, its abstemious consumption of fuel being perfectly suited to the depressed post-war conditions, but the home market dictated its early demise in 1922 – a year which turned out to be one of the worst in the American motorcycle industry's short history.

As the 1920s began, Henry Ford's master plan to swamp the country in a tidal wave of black Model Ts was already well advanced. Waking up to the threat, the other big players in the US auto industry launched a counterwave of competing econo-cars. This was all very bad news for the bike firms, whose fortunes immediately nosedived as precipitously as Ford's had soared. The problem was that the role of motorcycling had suddenly

changed from that of essential transport provider into a far less crucial one based on leisure. The sea-change was partly attributable to the bike manufacturers' own realignment towards competition in the mid-1910s. Many of Harley-Davidson's older and wiser employees predictably saw this as a belated vindication of Harley's much-criticised pre-war position on non-involvement. Nobody had foreseen the threat from Ford, nor the transformation it wreaked on the world of transport; accordingly, nobody had made any plans to reposition the motorcycle in the marketplace.

Ironically enough, Harley-Davidson's race team were by this stage breaking records at board and oval meetings all over the country, including the posting of the first ever 100mph-plus team victory at the Fresno, California track in early 1921. The 'Crew' also won the fifth Dodge City 300 Mile event in that same year. But the parlous economic conditions, combined with the futility (and expense) of attempting national domination over the still-strong Indian and Excelsior-mounted opposition, finally forced H-D to pull out of racing altogether at the end of 1921. The announcement was made by President Davidson in a circular release to Harley dealers: 'We find that we have become engaged in two distinct businesses at the factory; one, the business of racing, with a complete separate organisation, and the other, the legitimate business of making and selling motorcycles.'

A ruthless program of cost-cutting came into immediate effect, not just in the racing department, whose staff were literally disowned in the middle of a race meeting, but right throughout the entire company. If H-D were badly off, Indian were in a terrible state, their 1920 production figure of 20,000 being slashed to less than 7000 the following year. Both firms somehow staggered through to 1922, albeit in a severely trimmed state.

To avoid further blood-letting, a truce was arranged between the two companies. Over lunch in New York's Astor Hotel, Arthur Davidson and Indian's general manager Frank Weschler agreed to standardise the prices of competing models, so as to kill off the potentially ruinous effects of price-cutting. Nowadays, such an arrangement would, if uncovered, be vilified under the heading of cartel price-fixing; in 1922, it was the natural solution to a simple problem, and one which allowed both parties to make sensible plans for the future without having to keep looking over each other's shoulders. These price-fixing meetings went on to become an indispensable annual appointment for the managers of Indian and Harley-Davidson.

Having established the rules of the game in the most gentlemanly fashion, the two motorcycling giants then went away to lay plans for each other's destruction. For their part, Harley-Davidson's sales strategy was based on the

Left: Legendary British ace Freddie Dixon had good cause to grin after yet another win (this time at the 1923 Clipstone Speed Trials) on his modded JD racer.

Right: Douglas Davidson (no relation), here pictured at Brooklands in July 1921, had achieved a place in the record books one year earlier by becoming the first British rider to top 100mph.

Below right: Freddie Dixon again, making one schoolboy's dream come true in 1921.

launch of the JD, a larger-engined version of the faithful 1000cc J V-twin. Although the 1200cc JD was primarily aimed at the heavy duty three-wheeler commercial market, which still persisted despite the car-induced demolition of the private sidecar market, the new motor's extra power struck a sympathetic chord among the new breed of enthusiast motorcyclists moving in to fill the vacuum left behind by the Model T defectors. In this connection, the '74' (the JD's capacity in cubic inches) was also a useful response to the Chief, Indian's highly capable and well-favored entry in the heavyweight stakes. Looking back, the 74 could certainly be deemed a success, as this engine size and type featured in the Harley-Davidson lineup right up to 1980, and thereafter (in Sporster format) until the present day.

Following the success of their talks the previous year, Arthur and Walter Davidson arranged another meeting with Indian's Frank Weschler in 1923. The subject this time was the ejection from H-D and Indian sales showrooms of all other motorcycling marques, such as Excelsior, Cleveland and Reading Standard. Although Weschler was reportedly less than keen on this idea, having enjoyed the benefits of business cooperation and personal friendships with the representatives of these 'second division' companies for many years, the Davidsons finally prevailed upon him to agree to their proposal. The aim was to establish true solus franchises; the human consequence of this ruthless scheme was, inevitably, the demise of many smaller makes.

Another consequence of this pact was the creation of conditions suitable for a consolidation of Harley-Davidson's position at home, in Europe, and even Japan, where they established a foothold to challenge Indian's already firmly rooted Tokyo-based operation. This Japanese connection would eventually result in the setting up of a Harley-producing subsidiary in the Ginza district, which was in fact the first motorcycle manufacturing plant in Japan. Given the state of enmity which now exists between Harley riders and the Japanese 'opposition,' it is extraordinary and not a little ironic to think that the first motorcycles to be built on a commercial basis in Japan were Harley-Davidsons sold under the Rikuo badge.

In the mid-1920s, the transportation demands of America's forces of law and order were such that firms could make a healthy contribution to their own balance sheets by securing contracts to supply police motorcycles. The vibration problem that was an inbuilt design fault of big V-twins led many police officers to prevail upon their employers to let them use the much

smoother four-cylinder offerings of Henderson and Ace. The 1924 disappearance of Ace from the motorcycling scene cut down the choice somewhat, and naturally aroused the interest of Harley-Davidson, who could see big potential sales in the offing for any firm willing to put up a viable alternative to the Henderson.

Recognising that they did not possess the in-house expertise to produce an all-new engine, H-D immediately employed Ace's now redundant chief design engineer, Everett DeLong, on a brief to come up with a cheap new four-cylinder unit. Working in secret, DeLong quickly penned what he and the few others who were privy to the project considered to be a commercially worthy design. Effectively two sleeved-down J 74 twins laid side by side, the DeLong motor seemed to meet H-D's criteria. Bill Davidson, however, was not convinced; using his power as the company's leading shareholder, he vetoed the project on the grounds that it would have been too expensive to produce. Shortly afterwards, DeLong left the company to work for Cleveland, and all traces of the stillborn four-cylinder Harley-Davidson were destroyed.

The founders thus had to content themselves with a simple cosmetic revamping of the justly popular but by then old-fashioned J. Their options were necessarily limited by the fact that the J was their only high-profile model throughout the period of 1922-1929, after the Sport Twin's extinction in 1922 and before the arrival of the 45 cubic inch (750cc) model D in 1929. The improvements made to the J included a few welcome modifications to the engine, specifically to the valvegear and lubrication system, which were enough to ensure continuing loyalty among the 74's large and devoted band of followers.

Another continuing trend, and a somewhat less pleasant topic for discussion at H-D board meetings, was the apparently inexorable waning of motorcycling's popularity in the mid 1920s. Harley-Davidson were obliged to move into the ancillary parts business because of the fact that so many of their suppliers were being forced into closure by the prevailing economic circumstances. Their total output of machines was running at pre-war levels, only around 12,000 bikes being built in 1924. Even so, that made Harley-Davidson the biggest American manufacturer, with Indian producing approximately half as many machines as H-D. The only other manufacturer of note, Excelsior, was running at about half Indian's capacity, relying heavily on its police sales of Henderson fours.

Left: Harleys were designed to run best on America's ultra straight freeways, but that didn't stop this 1920's group from tackling the crookedest street in San Francisco.

Right: From 1922, the 1000cc 'J' had a big brother, the 1200cc 'JD'. Gray had turned to olive by then too.

Below: The 350cc Peashooter, available in both side valve and ohv formats, was campaigned on American tracks to great effect by Joe Petrali.

In 1925, Indian and Cleveland attempted to revitalise their flagging fortunes by launching lightweight single-cylinder bikes of 21 cubic inch (350cc) capacity. This engine size was extremely popular in England, home of the world's biggest motorcycle market at that time, so the American firms' decision to try and break into that field was a logical one. Equally predictable was Harley-Davidson's response the following year, in the shape of two separate 350cc singles. Model A was a sidevalve plodder capable of around 50mph (assuming that the piston could be persuaded to hold together at such a giddy speed). Model B differed in that it featured overhead valvegear, which endowed it with a considerably higher and more reliably obtainable top end of around 65mph.

The Harley dealership network, bred on a steady diet of fast V-twins, was less than enthusiastic about the new singles. But, after cynically dubbing the bikes 'Peashooters,' the same dealers were later required to eat their words. Although sales success was not instant in the US, where riders were not especially bothered about the 350's economy (its most obvious selling point), its race successes in the national series specially created for this class

Previous page: A long-track specification overhead valve Harley racer of the Great War period.

Left: Swedish daredevil Erik Westerberg did 104mph on his Harley on the ice of Stockholm's Edsviken Bay – without studs or spikes. . .

Below: Speedway was a popular sport in England in the late 1920s. Harley's Peashooter variant (foreground) had its work cut out against BSAs like the background example.

Right: Motorcycle sport of all kinds was incredibly well supported in the 1920s. This hillclimbing Harley sidecar entry looks like a family affair.

of machine were more difficult to ignore. The heroic feats of Joe Petrali on America's new 'flat track' circuits and on the notorious 'widowmaker' hill climbs were to assure him of a position of honor in the annals of Peashooter and, indeed, Harley-Davidson history.

Pressing home their advantage, H-D delighted their big twin fans with the announcement in 1927 of the JH (61ci) and JD-H (74ci) variants, scheduled for production in 1928. The most notable and attractive feature of these new roadburners was the utilisation of twin camshafts to operate the valves. Although aimed at the very top end of the market, with a suitably lofty price ticket nearly 20 percent higher than that of the ordinary J, the twin cammers were sufficiently impressive machines to earn themselves the reputation as the best Harleys ever made. It was unfortunate that the factory chose to wait so long before indulging itself in such a commendable upgrading exercise, since the worthy but venerable J was by this time fast reaching the end of its run.

There was about to be a major shakeup in the Harley range, in fact, with the launch of two new models in 1929 and 1930. The first new model was destined to underwrite the company's future for the next twenty years; the second one nearly damaged the company's reputation beyond repair.

And in between the two launches, events on Wall Street threatened to bring about the ruin not just of Harley-Davidson, but of every other company, corporation and conglomerate in the industrialised world.

Faced with this bleak outlook, and having only a couple of years before purchased a massive new plant on Capitol Drive in Wauwatosa, Wisconsin, in anticipation of an increase in sales which was suddenly looking less and less likely, Harley-Davidson took the unusual step of petitioning the US Government's Tariff Commission in 1951, requesting that a 40 percent import tax be imposed on all non-American motorcycles coming into the country. The petition was fiercely contested by the well-organised British Motorcycle Dealers Association, and ultimately sunk by testimony from Alfred Rich Child, one of the many disaffected ex-Harley dealers who had been on the receiving end of bullying treatment from the company in the past.

Having thus been forced to recognise that the only way to beat the Limeys was to compete with them on their own terms, Harley-Davidson entered into a new phase. The last surviving member of the original four founders, Arthur Davidson, had been killed on the day before New Year's Eve, 1950, the victim (with his wife) of an accident involving a speeding car. Although it would be untrue to say that the last traces of conservatism died with Davidson, it is certainly true that the early 1950s were busy years for H-D.

To start with, the old flathead 74 production line was finally closed down in 1952, after a four-year winding down period during which it was available only on special order by impecunious police forces outside America. At the same time, the 23-year history of the D model (the 45) was brought to a halt. Foot-operated gearshifts and conventional hand clutches were now included in the catalog, although only as an option to the foot clutch and tank-mounted gearlevers which were still standard equipment.

A new 750cc (45ci) middleweight was unveiled in the same year, featuring the foot change and hand clutch as standard. But that wasn't all. There was also suspension front and rear, and unit construction (engine and transmission in one housing) in the style of the successful British bikes. Lest Harley observers should faint at the sight of all this new technology, the new bike's flathead engine was reassuring evidence that the boys at Milwaukee had not gone completely mad.

This new middleweight, Harley's definitive answer to the foreign invaders, was assigned the letter K. It was accompanied in the catalog by a racing version, the KR, which was to take over from the flagging WR. Styling was clean and contemporary; everything looked right, in fact.

But then, the new wonderbikes went on sale.

Right: The racing KR series ran alongside the Ks, even when they were still sidevalvers like these '55 examples. The advent of the ohv versions helped to turn H-D's racing fortunes around.

Below: Another shot of the early KR sidevalve racer, complete with fender pad to allow the rider to adopt a wind-cheating posture.

New Models and Economic Problems

That Harley-Davidson should so regularly have been able to release such palpably imperfect new models as the K for public consumption, while still somehow managing to retain such a loyal hard core following, is a topic which almost merits a separate volume of its own. If nothing else, it is certainly eloquent testimony to the marque's magnetic appeal.

As has already been mentioned, the 1952 K looked right. It undoubtedly represented a quantum leap forward from the uninspiring twenties styling of the D it was meant to replace. The powerplant was a letdown, however. Although its unit construction gave it a modern facade, the mundane sidevalve format marked it down as very much the son of its father. Norton, along with a whole host of equally successful road and race machines from Italy, had proved the inherently superior power-producing capabilities of the overhead valve arrangement. Harley-Davidson themselves had sixteen years of ohv experience with the 61 and 74 big twins, but for the 45ci K they still elected to go down what was evidently expected to be an even safer flathead route.

It should have been a safer path. Extraordinary though it may seem, despite all the lessons learned in the past, the Harley engineers still had not cottoned on to the importance of proper product development. The KR racing version fell victim to early problems in the clutch department, notwithstanding the fact that its engine was actually no more powerful than its established predecessor, the WR. The straight K was revealed to be disappointingly sluggish, hard pressed to hit a top speed of 80mph. With a posted output of no more than 30bhp, it was patently lacking in the kind of lugging power demanded by those touring riders who preferred to travel two-up with luggage.

The K also suffered from its share of mechanical niggles, most notably a tendency to break gear teeth. Tuning parts were available to hoist the performance up to a more satisfactory level, and there were a few KK models produced in 1953, created by the insertion of the KR's hotter cams, polished ports and ball bearing crank into the K streetbike. By all accounts, these KKs were everything that the ordinary Ks should have been.

1953, Harley's 'Golden Anniversary' year, was celebrated with a bang: K panniers could now be ordered in the wonder material of white plastic, as well as in the usual fringed leather. In spite of this and many other anniversary temptations, the Ks continued to languish on showroom floors, kept company only by a larger version of the DKW-derived 125cc Hummer two-stroke. This, the new Teleglide, displaced 165cc, and sat in a chassis featuring rudimentary telescopic forks. The new machine rekindled a smoldering interest in the small strokers, and led to the reintroduction of the 125 in 1955. Both machines then ran alongside one another in the range up to and including 1959.

The lightweight end of H-D's range might have looked reasonably healthy, but by 1954, it was painfully obvious to all – including Harley's management – that the 750cc K was desperately in need of more power. This was achieved by the commonly-used Harley expedient of lengthening the stroke by three-quarters of an inch, to give a new displacement of 54ci (883cc). The new model, designated KH, also benefitted from revisions to the clutch and transmission, and breathed more easily through larger valves. Again, there was a street/racer hybrid, the KHK, and again, this was considered to be *the* K model to buy, if only because the 'racing' innards endowed it with performance to trade punches with quite ordinary imported sports machines.

Although it may not have seemed so at the time, the launch in 1970 of the FX 'Super Glide' can now be viewed as one of the most momentous events in Harley-Davidson's history. The 74 cubic inch (1200cc) 'Glide', a simple amalgam of the XL Sportster's front end and the FL frame/engine package, was offered in kick-start (FX) and electric start (FXE) options. Its singular plainness, as evidenced by the total lack of Electra Glide-type bodywork, was the very feature which made it so unusual. It represented the factory's first recognition of the fact that there were other kinds of H-D rider other than the straight-backed mature clubmen whom it had up to then fondly imagined to be its exclusive clientele.

Brainchild of the design department's Willie G Davidson (son of Chief Executive William H Davidson, and unquestionably the highest-profile 'biker' on the board), the FX was a perfect base machine for customising. This practice, previously regarded with a kind of sniffy hauteur by H-D, had been so facilitated by the explosion of aftermarket parts outlets, and so glamorised by motion pictures such as *Easy Rider*, that it had become virtually impossible to ignore. On the somewhat grudging basis of 'if you can't beat 'em, join 'em,' H-D had finally locked into the populist groove which was destined to steer them through the murky waters ahead. Later on, in the 1980s, the company's conversion in this direction was completed by their wholehearted entry into the immensely profitable arena of 'factory approved' custom parts and accessories.

Back in 1970, meanwhile, a new corporate logo had been created. It featured a prominent figure '1' and referred to Harley-Davidsons as 'The All-American Freedom Machines,' but problems on the production line in AMF's first few months of command turned this proud boast into a sick joke for a large number of dealers and customers. An integral part of AMF's crusade to wrench H-D into the twentieth century was a determination to crank the line up to automobile speed; unfortunately, this plan was at severe odds with the existing production facilities in Milwaukee. There was simply not enough time, space or technology in the Juneau Avenue works to meet the doubled targets newly set by AMF's line controllers. Quality control went out of the window as staff worked feverishly to build over 50,000 motorcycles a year. Many experienced workers had had enough and quit in disgust, further exacerbating the problems.

The atmosphere in the factory was at an all-time low. Out in the country, H-D dealers were aghast at the state of some of the machines they were receiving from the factory. And of course, as usual, they were the ones who were obliged to spend time and money making those machines saleable. In many cases, the bikes were so appallingly put together that they could not be made to work at all. In the final analysis, it took over two years to put matters to rights, by which time it had become a positive stigma to be seen running an 'AMF Harley'. Even now, bikes built in this era tend to be shunned by buyers in the secondhand market.

In 1971, in the midst of the quality scandal, AMF attempted to bring order to the situation by transferring a large part of the assembly process to one of their existing factory premises in York, Pennsylvania. Engines and transmissions continued to be built at the Capitol Drive works in Milwaukee, and then trans-shipped to York for mating with the chassis and cycle parts. Two years later, in 1973, the historic Juneau Avenue facility became a warehouse-cum-office complex. The severing of old links had been tragically underlined in August of '71 with the death of William J Harley, son of founder Bill Harley, and less traumatically by the resignation from the Vice Presidency of Walter Davidson Jr, nephew of Arthur Davidson.

1971 was a big year for the Sportster, in every sense. The XL motor was taken out to the 61ci (1000cc) size which many pundits had said it should have displaced from the start. The extra power thus created was to some extent vitiated by the commensurate increase in the amount of heat and vibration generated. It also further highlighted the shortcomings of the four-speed transmission, with its sticky action and its big jump in ratios from third to top. This latter expedient, intended to provide reasonable smoothness at the 55mph freeway speed limit, only did so at the expense of tractability in town. It was to be some years before H-D would properly address this question.

By 1973, Harley president William H Davidson decided he had had enough and retired, to be replaced by John O'Brien, one of AMF's production experts. A drive to weed out the less dynamic H-D dealers ensued, the idea being to put the company in a better position to defend itself from the rapidly growing Japanese threat. Fuelled by what turned out to be a false dawn in America's economic outlook, production was by then running at record levels, with over 70,000 motorcycles built in 1973 alone. The quality control

difficulties were still blighting the company's image, however. AMF supervisors on the shop floor were becoming increasingly frustrated by their inability to change the customs and practices of decades.

Behind their desks, the AMF directors were also becoming increasingly convinced that they had bought a pig in a poke, a dry and empty hulk which had already had all the profitability squeezed out of it by successive generations of the Harley and Davidson dynasties. Even though vast sums of money had been pumped in by AMF, there seemed to be no way of turning the company back out of the cul-de-sac into which it had been driven by H-D's over-cautious model policy. The FLs had become expensive anachronisms in a marketplace newly populated by Japanese mega-tourers of superior performance, such as Honda's Gold Wing. The Sportster was likewise being ridiculed by mold-breaking superbikes such as Kawasaki's 900cc Z1. Worse still, the Middle Eastern oil-producing nations had hoisted the price of crude to a level which was suddenly threatening the viability of all heavy industrial concerns, Harley-Davidson among them.

While considering their next move, AMF began recruiting engineers to work on H-D's listing ship. One of those engineers, Vaughn Beals, found himself lashed to the helm. By the end of 1977, his view from the bridge was daunting, to say the least. Annual production had dropped back down to 45,000 from a '76 figure of 61,000; a new Sportster variant, the XLCR Cafe Racer, had bombed in the showrooms; and there was a strong suspicion that the big four Japanese firms were 'dumping' their excess production on the American market, undercutting H-D by discounting their bikes to incredibly low price levels.

In 1978, AMF paid heavily for the luxury of testing this suspicion in front of the government's Tariff Commission. As had happened in 1951, H-D's case was effectively killed off by testimony from their own dealers, who gave vent to many years' worth of pent-up bile by denigrating Harley's regressive attitude in regard to model development and other matters. As had happened in 1951, the Commission listened closely to the damning evidence before throwing out H-D's claim of unfair Japanese competition.

Left: Late 80s Evolution-engined FXRS Low Rider is arguably the best all-round Harley street bike yet.

Right: Believe it or not, this 'hogged out' drag-racer style 93-incher started off life as a police bike.

Below right: Highest profile descendant of the founders still working for the old firm is Willie G Davidson. He has masterminded the styling changes which have revolutionised sales in recent years.

Left: 1987 Softail Custom married traditional hardtail look with the convenience of hidden suspension.

Right: Harleys are now finding their way into the garages of well-heeled professional types. . .

Below right: . . .as well as into the hearts of true enthusiasts who mortgage their houses to buy one.

Below: HOG (Harley Owners Group) liaises with factory on product policy matters.

Licking their wounds, AMF's bosses fell back in a disorderly retreat to the bread and butter business of selling – or attempting to sell – motorcycles. To rekindle some interest in the ancient FL, its engine size was increased to the old sidevalver's capacity of 80 cubic inches (around 1340cc). By 1980, all the FLs and FXs were powered by this motor, killing off the once-classic 74ci/1200cc class (the 1200 would actually return to the range in the late 1980s, but only in the Sportster's unit construction format). A much more welcome step forward was the provision of a five-speed transmission on the 1980 FLT tourer, an advance which combined with vibration-isolating engine and footboard mounts to make this the most relaxed cruiser ever to bear the H-D badge.

Further evidence of the company's new-found commitment to enhanced rider comfort was to be found on the 1980 Sturgis, a new variation on the 'stripped-look' FX theme. Named after the annual bike rally venue in the Dakota hills, the all-black Sturgis was distinguished by its toothed-belt final drive. The claim that this would provide up to 50,000 miles of lubrication-free, adjustment-free motorcycling was not always borne out, and there were additional complications attendant upon the replacement procedure, but the Kevlar-reinforced Gates belt undoubtedly made a noticeable contribution to the FX's quietness and smoothness in operation. The Sturgis and the FLT, both of which were benchmark machines in their own way, had been designed by Erik Buell. A talented engineer, Buell subsequently left H-D to set up his own business producing purposeful XR1000-based specials aimed at the 'Battle of the Twins' races, first instituted at Daytona in the mid 1980s.

1980 was the crunch year for AMF. Cutting their losses, and having failed to find a suitable outside buyer, they offered Harley-Davidson up to a management-led buyout group headed by Vaughn Beals. Following lengthy negotiations throughout 1980 and the early part of 1981, the handover was finally completed on 1 June 1981, with Beals becoming the new Chairman. Reaffirming his commitment to the principle of combining the best aspects of the old and the new, Beals set out on the long and uphill road towards re-establishment of Harley's once-great name.

The journey began, symbolically at least, with an organised ride by members of the new management from the York assembly plant (which had been given over to the buyout group by AMF as part of the deal) to the Milwaukee engine-building facility. The last echoes of the takeover hullabaloo had only just died down when the cold shadow of economic recession fell across Harley's portals – not for the first time. Inflation was eroding the saleability of H-D's products from one side, while the continued landing of massive quantities of Japanese motorcycles in American ports was chipping great lumps out of their customer base. Discounting was once again rife, but even the

truly desperate discounting measures taken by the Japanese to reduce their massive overstocking in the States proved inadequate.

H-D were hit very hard at this time. Hundreds of workers had to be laid off as domestic sales all but dried up. A new stripped-to-the-bone Sportster, the XLX-61, was released with a bargain price tag of just $3995 in an attempt to stimulate some showroom action, and streamlined new 'materials as needed' (MAN) production line techniques were brought into force. This latter move gave rise to real financial benefits in the longer term, and to increased worker contentment in the short and long terms. But the short term financial benefits were not so easily gained. The company's financial position was still parlous.

So it was that in early 1983, Harley-Davidson were obliged to petition the Tariff Commission for a third time in search of relief from the damaging effects of cheap Japanese imports. Much preparatory effort went into ensuring that their case would seem more reasoned than it had on the two previous abortive occasions. Rather than tarring all Japanese motorcycles

Every February, thousands of motorcycling enthusiasts from all over the world congregate in Daytona, Florida. Ostensibly, the event is a week long series of road races held inside the Daytona speedbowl, but in practice the vast majority of spectators are there for the social scene, to cruise downtown bars. . . or simply to watch one another.

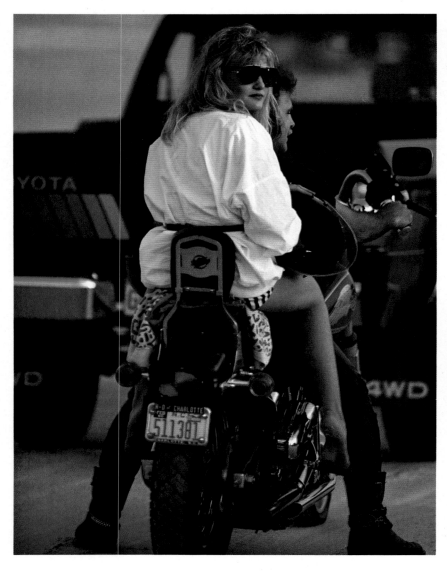

Selected Specifications

	JD/JDH 61 & 74 cu.in.	61-E	Hydra-Glide	XL Sportster	Duo-Glide	Electra-Glide	FX Super Glide
First Year of Manufacture	1928	1936	1949	1957	1958	1965	1971
Engine Type	Twin Cam	Knucklehead	Panhead	XL-Shovel	Panhead	Panhead (1965) Shovelhead (1966 on)	Shovelhead
Capacity	1000/1200cc	1000cc	1200cc	883cc	1200cc	1200cc	1200cc
Bore and Stroke (inches)	3.31×3.50/ 3.41×3.50	3.31×3.50	3.43×3.96	3.00×3.81	3.43×3.96	3.43×3.96	3.43×3.96
Horsepower Rating (claimed)	8.68hp/9.5hp	40bhp	55bhp	40bhp	55bhp	60bhp	65bhp
Transmission	3 speed	4 speed	4 speed	4 speed	4 speed	4 speed	4 speed
Weight (wet)	575lbs	600lbs	600lbs	500lbs	600lbs	780lbs	575lbs
Top Speed (est)	90mph	98mph	100mph	85mph	100mph	97mph	99mph

	XR 750 (Alloy)	FXS Low Rider	FLT Tour Glide	FXB Sturgis	FXRS Low Glide	FXST Softail
First Year of Manufacture	1972	1978	1980	1980	1982	1985
Engine Type	XL-Shovel	Shovelhead	Shovel/Evo	Shovelhead	Shovel/Evo	Evolution
Capacity	750cc	1200cc	1340cc	1340cc	1340cc	1340cc
Bore and Stroke (inches)	3.12×2.98	3.43×3.96	3.50×4.25	3.50×4.25	3.50×4.25	3.50×4.25
Horsepower Rating (claimed)	90bhp	65bhp	65bhp	65bhp	65bhp	65bhp
Transmission	4 speed	5 speed	5 speed	4/5 speed	5 speed	4 speed
Weight (wet)	320lbs	640lbs	795lbs	630lbs	640lbs	650lbs
Top Speed (est)	130mph	100mph	98mph	100mph	102mph	108mph

Left: The ultimate expression of luxury touring – the FLT Tour Glide.

Index

Page numbers in *italics* refer to illustrations

Accessories, accessory market 52
Ace motorcycles 26
Aermacchi company 70, 72
  Ala Verde 250cc four-stroke single
    63, 70, 72
  Ala Verde 350cc four-stroke 72, 85
  Leggero M-50 50cc two-stroke 72
  Rapido 125cc 72
  SS, SX range 125, 175, 250cc 72, *82*
American Machine and Foundry Co
  78, 82, 85, 87-8, 90
American Motor Cycle Association
  (AMA) 43, 52, 57, 85
Ariel company 54
  Red Hunter motorcycle 54
Armstrong motorcycle specialists 99
Aster car company, Paris 12

Bangor Punta company 78
Barth Manufacturing Company 12
Beals, Vaughn *87*, 88, 90
Bouton, Georges 12
Boyd, Glen 22
Brando, Marlon 57
British Motor Cycle Dealers
  Association 60
Brooklands *13*, *25*, *27*
BSA company 54
BSA motorcycles *32*, 54
Buell, Erik 90

Cagiva company, Italy 72
Californian Highway Patrol 42, 95
Capitol Drive, Milwaukee, plant 60,
  85, 87
Child, Alfred Rich 60
Cleveland company and motorcycles
  26, 29
Clipstone Speed Trials, 1923 *26*
Cunningham, Walter 22
Cushman company scooters 54
customizing *68-9*, 69-70, 87, *102-5*

Davidson, Arthur 10, 12, 13, 14, 15,
  22, 24, 26, 42, 60, 87
Davidson, Douglas *27*
Davidson, Walter *11*, 12, 13, 14, 15,
  24, 26, 42, 45, 52
Davidson, Walter, Jr 87
Davidson, William A 15, 26, 50
Davidson, Willie G 87, *89*, 99
Davidson, William H 52, 87
Daytona Beach *59*, *63*, *68*, *84*, *106-8*
  mile record at 48
de Dion, Count Albert 12
de Dion-Bouton engine 12
DeLong, Everett 26
disk brakes 76
Dixon, Freddie *26-7*
Dodge City racetrack 22, 24
drag racing, drag strips 69
du Pont, E Paul 42
Ducati motorcycles 72

Easy Rider, film *56*, 87
electric starter 76
engines,
  Knucklehead 48, 57
  Panhead *54-6*, 57-8, 76, 78
  Shovelhead *70*, 78
  V2 Evolution 6, 95, *5*, 99
  V-twin 6, 15, *15*, 18, *19*, 21, 43, 48,
    78, 85
Evinrude, Ole 12
Excelsior company 18, 42
  motorcycles 24, 26, 36

Federation of American Motorcyclists
  15
Flying Merkel company 18
  see also Ohio motorcycles
Fonda, Peter *56-7*
Ford, Henry 22, 24
Ford cars, Model T 24, 26
Fowler, Rem 15
freeway forks 6
Fresno, California, racetrack 24
front brakes 36, 38

Gable, Clark *50*
gearbox, two-speed 22
Gott, Rodney C 78

Harley, William J 45, 52, 87
Harley, William S 10, *10*, 12, 13-14,
  15, 22, 45, 52, 87
Harley Owners Group *90*, 95
Harley-Davidson company 10, 15, 50,
  58
  and Aermacchi share purchase 70,
    76
  and AMA 52, 85
  under AMF ownership 82, 85, 87-8,
    90
  Armstrong takeover 99
  and customising 87
  dealer network 22, 24, 29, 42, 54,
    57, 60, 69-70, 87, 88
  in Depression 33, 42, 43, 50
  financial difficulties of 1965-7 76, 78
  foundation of company 10, 12
  Holiday Rambler Motorhome Group
    bought 99
  and Indian
    dealer agreement with 26
    price agreements with 24, 42
    rivalry with 42, 43, 50
  and motorcycle sport 21, 22, 24, 43,
    85
  1980s problems 90
  requests for import tax 60, 90, 95
  scooter experiment 72
  Trihawk Company bought 99
  USN munitions contract 99
  in World War I 24
  in World War II 52, 54
Harley-Davidson motorcycles (*the
  year indicating first appearance of
  the series*),
  1903 400cc 12-13, 15
    420cc version 14
  1909 5-35 575cc (35ci) *12*, 15, 24
    F V-twin version 15,18
  1911 J 1000cc (61ci) *17-19*, 24, 26,
    29, 33, 40, 42
  1914 11K racer 22
  1919 Model W 37ci 'Sport Twin'
    23-4, 24, 26
  1922 JD 1200cc (74ci) 26, *26*, 29
  1924 planned DeLong four-cylinder
    26
  1925 Model A 350cc (21ci) side

valve *28*, 29, 33, 54
  1925 Model B 350cc (21ci) ohv *28*,
    29, 33, 54
  1929 Model C 500cc (30.5ci) 33,
    36, 38, 43, 54
  1929 Model D 750cc (45ci) 26, 33,
    36, 38, 40, 42, *42*, 43, 48, 52,
    54, 60, 64
    1937 version 50
  1929 VL 1200cc (74ci) 33, 38, *41*,
    42, 48, 50, 64
  1936 VLH 43
  1932 Three-wheel Servi-cars 38, *41*,
    42, *53*, 55, 76
  1936 Model E 61-E Knucklehead
    1000cc (61ci) *34-5*, 43, *44-5*, 45,
    48, *49*, 50, 54, 57, 64, 109
  1937 UL 74ci side-valve twin 50, 54,
    64
    ULH 80ci 50
  1937 DLDR 750cc Class C racer 50
  1939 WLA *37*, *48-9*, *51*, 52
    WLB, WLC 52
    WLR 50
    WR 60, 64
  1940 F series 74ci big twin 50, 59,
    70
  1958 FL Duo Glide 58, *58*, *65*, 85,
    88, 90, 109
  1965 FL/FLH Electra Glide 64,
    72-5, 76, *77*, 78
  1980 FLT Tour Glide *75*, 90, *108*,
    109
  1942 XA 750cc side valve 52
  1947 Model M ('Hummer') 125cc
    two-stroke *53*, 54
  1953/55 165/125cc Teleglide 64
  1949 'Hydra Glide' 58, 99, 109
  1949 Panhead *54-6*, 57-8, 67, 76,
    78
  1952 K series 750cc (45ci) 60, 64,
    67
    KH 883cc (54ci) *58*, 64, 67, 76
    KK 64
    KL 67
    KR series 60, *61*, 64, *66*, 76, 85
  1957 XL Sportster 6, 26, *66*, 67, 69,
    70, 76, 78, *83*, *85*, 87, 88, *93-4*,
    109
    XLCR1000 Cafe Racer 38, *81*, *86*,
      88
    XLCH, XLH 69
    XLR racer *68*
  1981 XLX-61 90, 95
  1983 XR1000 95, 99
  1960 Topper 165cc Scooter 72
  1966 Shovelhead 74ci *70*, 78
  1972 XR 750 dirt track cycle *7*, 76,
    76, *78-9*, 85
  1970s SX (Aermacchi) two-stroke *82*
  1970 FX Super Glide 1200cc (74ci)
    84, *86*, 87, 109
  1980 FX Sturgis 90, 109
  1982 FXRS Sport Glide *85*, 88, 95,
    109
  1984 FXSTS Springer Softail *98*, 99,
    109
  1986 Heritage Softail *94*, 99, *99*
Harley-Davidson team, the 'Crew' 24
Hedstrom, Oskar 13
Hendee, George 13, 14, 22
Henderson motorcycles (Excelsior)
  26, 42
  1914 four-cylinder *20*, 26
hillclimbing *33*
Holiday Rambler Motorhome Group
  bought 99
Hollister, California, weekend
  incidents in 57
Honda Gold Wing motorcycle 88
Hoover, President Herbert 42

Idler mechanism introduced 21
Indian company 14, 18, 21, 24, 26,
  29, 42, 50
  motorcycles,
    1902 model 13, 14
    1914 eight-valve models 22
    1920 V-twin *21*
    Chief 26, 43, 50
    'Dispatch-Tow' three-wheeler 42
    'Iron Redskin' range 50
insignia, Harley-Davidson *100-101*
Isle of Man TT races 15, 21

Japan 43
  H-D operations in 26, 38, *41*
  imports from 70, 88, 90, 95

Kawasaki motorcycles 95
  Z1 900cc 88
Kramer, Stanley 57
Kruger, Emil 12

Laconia 100-mile Road Race, 1947 *47*
Lindbergh, Charles *39*
lubrication systems 26, 40, 50, 52,
  57

McLay, James 14
Marshall Plan 54
Mervin, Lee 57
Mork, Fred *63*
motorcycle sport *9*, 15, 21, 22, 29,
  32-3, 33, 43, 85

National Motor Museum, Beaulieu,
  England *48-9*
Norton company 54, 64
Norton motorcycles,
  1907 Peugeot-engined 15
  International 43

Manx 58, *59*

O'Brien, John 87
Ohio 980cc Flying Merkel V-twin *14*
Ottaway, William 22, 50, 52
overhead valve systems 45, 64, 67

Petrali, Joe 33, 48, 49 (cap.)
police motorcycles 22, 26, 42, 50,
  52-3, 95
Porsche company 95

Rayborn, Cal 85, *85*
Reading Standard motorcycles 26

Servi-car/Dispatch-Tow cycles 42-3
sidecars 22, 26, *33*, 40, 76
Sifton, Tom 43
silencing 15
'Silent Gray Fellow' sobriquet *12*, 15,
  24
springer forks 36, 58, *96-7*, 99
Springsteen, Jay *78-9*
Stockholm, Edsviken Bay *32*
suspension 58, 60, 69, 78

Tancrede, Babe *47*
tele-hydraulic front forks 58, 99
Temple, Claude *25*
Thor Motorcycle group 22
  'White Thor' racers 22